A Caterpillar's Story

WRITTEN BY
ALYCE PARK BRESHEARS

ILLUSTRATED BY
PAISLEY HANSEN

Copyright 2014, Alyce Park Breshears

All rights reserved.

No part of this book may be reproduced or shared by any electronic or mechanical means, including but not limited to printing, file sharing, and email, without prior written permission from Fideli Publishing.

ISBN: 978-1-60414-788-9

Translated by Tony Campbell

I am a Caterpillar.

My name is Casandra Sui Lin Consuelo.

Soy una oruga.

Me llamo Casandra Sui Lin Consuelo.

Alyce Park Breshears

My body is a bit long,

but I can move about on trees, plants, leaves

and I really love to eat milk weed.

Mi cuerpo es un poco largo,

pero puede moverse en los árboles, las plantas,

las hojas y me encanta comer malezas leche.

Alyce Park Breshears

I eat all day long.

Something inside my body tells me this is what I must do to survive.

Also I must keep moving to stay away from those

that would like to have me for their dinner.

Yo como todo el día.

Algo dentro de mi cuerpo me dice que esto es lo

que tengo que hacer para sobrevivir. También debo

seguir moviéndose para mantenerse alejado

de los que le gustaría tenerme para su cena.

Alyce Park Breshears

Again, there is a movement inside me that tells me

to start making a bed that will be soft.

My bed is called a cocoon.

It will keep me warm and enable me to change into my new body.

Una vez más, hay un movimiento dentro de mí que me dice

para empezar a hacer una cama que sea suave.

Mi cama se llama un capullo.

Se me va a mantener el calor y me permitirá cambiar a mi nuevo cuerpo.

Alyce Park Breshears

I will hang from a branch of a tree

or even a large plant and go to sleep.

Voy a ser capaz de respirar y esperar a que el tiempo de

mi cuerpo me dice que despertar.

Me colgare de una rama de un árbol

o aun una planta grande y me dormire.

Voy a ser capaz de respirar y esperar a que el tiempo de

mi cuerpo me dice que despertar.

Alyce Park Breshears

I will not be the same as before. It will be a wonderful awakening and I will be able to do so many other things that I have admired in other insects. I am an insect. I have six legs.

I do not speak or let you know where I am.

I wish I could tell you what it will be like for me.

No sere como era anteriormente. Sera un despertamiento admirable y podre hacer muchas cosas que he admirado en otros insectos.

Soy un insecto. Tengo seis patas.

No hablo ni le dejo saber donde estoy.

Quisiera poder decirle como sera para mi.

Alyce Park Breshears

I will have wings! I can fly!

And I am no longer considered an ugly green caterpillar,

because I have changed into a butterfly.

I am as pretty as the beautiful flowers.

I have different colors on my wings. They are bright and colorful.

Voy a tener alas! ¡Puedo volar! Y ya no estoy considerado una oruga

verde feo, porque me he convertido en una mariposa.

Yo soy tan bonita como las hermosas flores.

Tengo diferentes colores en las alas. Son luminosas y coloridas.

Alyce Park Breshears

I will remain a butterfly.

There is no going back to being a caterpillar.

Me quedare una mariposa.

No hay vuelta de nuevo a ser una oruga.

Alyce Park Breshears

It is so wonderful to have wings.

I can see all around me. I must go now, and visit all the flowers I can.

Es maravilloso tener alas. Puedo ver todo alrededor de mi.

Ahora tengo que irme, y visitar todas las flores que puedo.

About the Author

Having grown up in the San Joaquin Valley of California where English and Spanish are spoken, I wrote a book so that speakers of both languages could enjoy the story.

About the Illustrator

Paisley Hansen is an art major at Ball State University and a freelance illustrator. "I've been drawing as long as I can remember, but I began illustrating children's books at 16 when I published my own book *Chubbi Bunni and the Pastry Shoppe* through Fideli Publishing," Paisley says. "I've been illustrating for Fideli's authors ever since and it's been a wonderful experience!" She is currently working toward a Bachelor of Fine Arts degree in animation and hopes to someday work on animated films and games.